NIGHT BUS TO MONTE CARLO

MARK WARD

Best wishes

Mark

2022

Tanya

NIGHT BUS TO MONTE CARLO

Selected & New

MARK WARD

Selected by Neil Rollinson

Editors: Neil Rollinson and Paul Farley

PENNILESS PRESS PUBLICATIONS
Website : www.pennilesspress.co.uk/books

First published
June 2022

ISBN   978-1-913144-37-1

By the author

Poetry
Thunder Alley
The Visitor's Book
Used Rhymes
Coleridge Street
Portrait in Black

Prose
A Guide to Historic Haworth & the Brontës

Dedicated to
Pamela Woof, and the late Dr Robert Woof
The Wordsworth Trust, Grasmere.

CONTENTS

No upright poem in its upright English can seem to me quite free from limescale under the rim.

Geoffrey Hill

A Question

When the ice-shelf shifts,
what's going to happen to
all the ornaments?

Junction 31

There may be a no smoking policy
but these Asian guys are usually okay?
All right if I smoke mate? Been a hell of a flight.
'No problem: been anywhere interesting?'
Kashmir, I tell him. He ponders a moment.
'Indian or Pakistan?' *Indian.*
'Aah…' We both fall silent and return.
I to the campfires, the saffron pickers,
and the Floating Gardens of Srinagar,
he to the daily shelling, the terror,
confusion, loss and enforced separation.
On the road, always moving; even now,
each long mile taking him further away.

It's Junction 31 mate. Almost home.

Haiku to the Fairground Goldfish

Clear plastic to black,
in usually less than
a week – Assured.

Mr Mercer leaves his Wife

The mealy-mouthed Mercer flies his kite,
when summer's luscious sparkling rain abates.
And the tarmac and the red brick and the slates,
are swilled and spilled with gold and silver light;
which shines on Mrs Mercer's polished face:
all buffed and waxed and plucked and pinched and preened.
She scowls and says, "The sun should know his place,
to shine so uninvited, on One he should esteem!"
Her husband, cowed, replied he couldn't say.
His soaring kite, whorled, wheeled and dipped and spun.
As she loathed him with a look and turned away,
Mr Mercer and the kite became as One.

He sees the sunlight liquefy his spouse,
and altitude reduce her, 'til at last:
she was a resin-coated insect – with his house
a lump of amber, set in a silver clasp.

Thunder Alley

i

Cycles.

Unprompted, he can casually dispense
a razor to the cheek of innocence,
carving his problems in his victim's face:
a white-bone pelmet; a sagging crimson drape.

Whenever he gets troubled, bored or stressed,
a gasbag brings him temporary oblivion.
The girl he meets is suitably impressed,
and he fucks her in the park by the pavilion.

At fifteen, she's pregnant with his child.
He gifts her a bracelet and some trainers:
ignores her when his hooded mates are round,
and kicks her for the slightest misdemeanour.

'Things will improve when the baby arrives,'
she tells herself, tasting his boot in her mouth.

ii

Home-grown.

It is important when passing through this life
to leave some record of one's journey.

Thomas Gray

Fairly straightforward, this martyrdom thing.
Blind faith: semtex and a ticket one-way.
Where to? Well that's entirely down to physics.

This elegy records his earthly stay.

He could have been a doctor or lawyer.
A teacher; someone held in high esteem.
He never realised his full potential.
Full many a flower was born to blush unseen.

His life was brief and unremarkable.
He died abroad with malice in his heart:
dispatched among the scorched and carbonised,
the guiltless amputees with shattered lives.
Formless; reduced to ounces, blood and fat
slather on the walls of a Tel-Aviv bar.

The Last Supper

Remember the 70s; the Skinheads,
the Sex Pistols, Carlos the Jackal,
mayhem on the terraces: the three-day week.
Picketing gravediggers, blackouts and bombs.
The I.R.A was toasting its success
while some poor bastard was getting his head
kicked in, for his simply being Irish;
and not for anything he'd done or said!
And spare a thought for Jimmy McGuerter.
On his way home with a fish supper in
the aftermath of Mountbatten's murder…

They punched and kicked him so hard that his head
burst open on the pavement like a ripe fruit.

His subsequent meals, ingested through tubes.

iv

Victimization

The fat kid with the jam-jars always copped
it. Or those too clever, beautiful or black;
or gay, or just plain different – their riposte;
to learn self-ridicule, or join the pack.
Those too shy or lacking self-esteem,
and often friends with whom they might confide,
could find each day a harrowing ordeal:
tormented to the verge of suicide.
And racism itself is non-exclusive.
The fat kid with the jam-jars understands.
As one we are generous and inclusive.
As tribes we seem by nature, partisan.

When our streets form galleries of commonwealth.
Through every painted frame you see yourself.

The Editor
For Paul Farley.

42 poems: *a modest collection*,
I told myself,
handing them over.

24 poems: *a pamphlet perhaps?*
He suggests
handing them back!

Landfill

Old Tom Barker down at the landfill,
slept with a fireguard over his head
to prevent the rats from chewing his lobes.
Had his whiskers bleached white by their urine instead,
as they to'd and fro'd across the bridge, spanning his face.

Uncle Jack washed his hair in paraffin
to prevent lice. To which it could be regarded
a success, as it also prevented hair growth.

Aunty Molly thought we'd sent a boatload
of gherkins to the Falklands. She always misheard.
When Lord Ha Ha said the Palace was a target.
She thought he meant *The Palace* where she worked.

Bernard died, but kept walking by Alice's window.
He wouldn't leave until she joined him – so she did.

Michael Dixon

Scrawny lad with orange hair (the type that
doesn't like the sun:) a keen fisherman,
he preferred the river bends to street corners
and bus shelters, where his mates would hang out.

When all hell broke loose in the nightclub and
he was singled out for 'a good kicking'
by the doormen, his skinny ribs couldn't take it.

He got through the night, but the next day on
the river, he started drifting –

                              down –

                                    down,

by the sloping banks of the long green water:
the hot blue lights and the black asphalt:
past the cool white sheets and hurried voices;
through the rising vapours at the distant bar;
and on – to the eternal sea beyond.

Spanish Lament

When I was a kid
they returned with sombreros.
Sangria and castanets;
lacquered lace fans.

Now it's a villa.
A Timeshare apartment.
Skin melanomas.
Booze and cheap fags.

The Mansion of Aching Hearts

At the former Union Workhouse on the hill,
they'd sit in soporific bliss and stare,
as slanted latticed sunbeams sloped, and spilling
through the windows, split the melancholy air.
Wayne Ruben squints, adjusts his stool,
lines the light-shaft with the table and bench.
Jane will dip her toes, then skirt the pool
of sun: dark shadows more familiar, less intense.

Now the restraining cells are silent, and the halls
where the sectioned were sedated, and observed,
echo no more with disillusioned souls,
the corridors no longer the preserve
of aching hearts, the dormitories now still;
at the former Union Workhouse on the hill.

Impulse

In the process of writing
my grant proposal, I
smoked some boogie-ball.

Out of focus – the words spread
across the page like bacteria,

and I found myself – unworthy.

Amusements

I made my money that day, on the Penny Falls,
when my carefully slotted penny brought
down the whole row: momentarily fused,
it crashed hard; like a lump of solid bronze.

Half a pound heavier, and feeling rich,
I made my way up to the Marina,
where a rather sad looking dolphin, waved,
chattered and leapt through hoops, for our amusement.

From there, the Reptile House and its star attraction;
two alligators – in touching distance
through the railings. Bored and uninspired,
they lay motionless by the shallow pool,
every inch of their backs covered in coins,
thrown by frustrated punters wanting action.

Sequined alligators – Now that's showbiz!

Church Candle

That night, he sacrificed himself for love.
Drawn to the naked flame in search of a mate,
he stumbled into a pool of hot wax,
and there – like a limed finch, he remained.

I found him the next morning: wings outstretched,
opaque; entombed in the central crater.

I re-lit the candle and released him.
Unbound, he floated brightly: his vivid
markings, a glazed umber and chestnut brown,
seemed to ripple in the soft bending light.

And so it continued each night,
                            until
the well deepened, the high walls collapsed, and
the moth; consumed within an avalanche
of molten wax
               – was ultimately redeemed.

November
i.m.   M. D. Ward

Nothing should grow here, I told myself,
easing my fingers through the thin crust of frost,
into the cold red sand of the fresh grave.

The earth was already compacting – good drainage
they said; though I try not to think about that!
I prefer using my hands to cold steel.
This was no autopsy; more like contact.
The impression of my fingers created
fluted fist-size earthenware bowls,
and into each I placed four bulbs – a nest.

This month I thought we'd keep each other company.
What else is there…? An answer phone message:
that look, you gave me at the hospital door:
and this red sand in my fingernails, I'm loath to remove.

You could be Anywhere?

It happens sometimes on really dark nights,
when the orange street lights of Pendle Drive
and Roman Road, seem to float. They remind
me of the fire-boats at anchor on the
Bosphorus: men frying fish in iron skillets.
Taking turns to come quayside with their catch.

Only the other day the morning sun
over Whiteburk, glared with such intensity,
I thought of the bush-fires in New South Wales,
and closed my window to keep out the smoke.

In a misty haze; the rumble of trucks
on Preston New Road is *Mosi O Tunya*,
The Smoke that Thunders; rising as vapour,
from the bowels of Victoria Falls.

Prosthetics

Ben ripped his nuts off, sliding down a flagpole.
Caught them on the cord-hook…Ouch!
You couldn't tell the difference when they gave him rubber ones.
Except they had a tendency to bounce.

An Eventful Night

I tell you, it's busy out there tonight!
People everywhere. See my mum as well,
having dinner with the boxing promoter
Don King – at the Sett End of all places?

Everything's real: nothing's impossible.
Even the blind man is seeing clearly,
while the deaf girl hears him whisper her name,
by the kissing-gate, where she rendezvous.

Yep, it sure is busy: yet oh so strange.
Everyone is familiar, yet somehow
out of place?

        Suddenly, seconds later,
there's not a soul about, and I'm clinging
to this ledge, a fingertip from safety,
wondering – Where the fuck is everyone?

The Ratchet
For Neil Rollinson

'What's this? Victoriana! I don't hear you
talk like that: It's wrong: get rid, it's out of place.
And tell me – What's with all the fucking adverbs?
This poem carries too much baggage mate!'

Kingfisher

Enchanted birds, kingfishers; and like water-sprites
seldom seen in these parts. Yet since I've taken
to walking with you, I've already seen
two: the last one only the other day.

More projectile than vertebrate, his long
beak gives him a severe countenance; this
is more than compensated by his bright
iridescent plumage: robes fit for a king.

We barely noticed the moorhen nearby:
Her modest down by comparison, seemed
quite drab: nor did we audibly gasp when
she shuffled nervously from the reed bed,
as when he flashed across the water like
phosphorous, alighting on the alder beside us.

Where sitting with you, in the late afternoon,
by the sloe-black river – everything was perfect.

Oh, and by the way…

I like you; I like the sound of your voice:
the deep resonance, of your earthy vowels.
Coarse, salty, yet familiar as the moist
dank air, and coal smoke seeping through rooftop cowls.

The Brewery's rancid yeasty breath exhales,
and mingles with the clipped consonants – no frills;
just calico, coal and raw cotton bales.
The filthy canal, a great sump for the mills.

Your abbreviated syntax feels like home.
Worn; uneven like the former cobbled lanes.
Hard-pressed forbears interred within the loam.

A broken iron downspout gulps and gurgles in the rain.

Your slow syllabic shuffle glides – and grapples
the larynx; through primary instinct, not choice:
the child, the fairground, the sweet toffee apples,
return and enrich, the sound of your voice.

Hellifield

Rarely seen rain like it!
Torrential: vertical.
Great globules, hurtling past
my window at high velocity:
shattering – dispersing in the road.

In its aftermath, a lull: silence,
the stillness after violence.

The air fills with the noise of water.
Accentuated by the high fells,
it carries the torn leaves with the dust and grime
of the last days of summer, through the culverts
and gullies to the barred jaws of the iron drains.

The meadow opposite is sodden and pale,
except for a small patch – noticeably richer,
where last year's stillborn lamb
had rotted in the corner of the field.
And I find myself going back – to the
tree-lined road to Hellifield.

The saplings have taken well, along
the ridges and slopes of the high embankments;
the bulldozed bulwarks that once concealed
the foot and mouth depot from the road.

Hellifield: burial ground of the slaughtered Danes.
Appropriated by the ministry for its despatch units.

Blood and bone: bone and ash.
It always comes down to this.

From my window the sky turns pallid,
as a grey drizzle enters the vale: its greyness
permeates the landscape,

and everything of beauty is made dull by it.

We were redirected through a neighbouring town
the night they set his cows on fire.
But they couldn't redirect the smoke.
Iron grey: sweet, nauseous; it drifted far into the evening.
I saw him later that night on the telly:
slumped on the fence like a beaten fighter.
He'd been that way since the final 'pop' of the bolt-gun.

Blood and bone: bone and ash.
It always comes down to this.

The squall returns, gusting, though
with less intensity: pellets of rain
bounce off the window: raindrops falling from
the overflowing gutter, splatter on the sill.

It continued throughout the summer.
Each day the bright red trucks – the carcass bearers,
would leave Hellifield for the farms, the pits, the pyres.
Returning each evening to swill out and disinfect.
The land, un-grazed, turned to wilderness.
The visitors didn't come: the vacancy signs stayed up.

The sky outside begins to brighten,
from mercury to silver then pale translucent blue;
delicate, fragile, reassuring.
Sheep resemble cotton grass on the high fells.
Cattle lounge in the low pasture.
Everything is so much clearer now.

There's a disused airfield to the north of here,
where the grass grows rich on fertile soil.
Beneath its surface, the matted hair and skeletal
remains of half a million sheep and cattle;
in each skull an identical hole, a finger's width.

Blood and bone: bone and ash.

The Beer Trap

For some it was regular
as taking out ashes.
A constitutional. A prayer.

Emptying the beer trap
was a daily occupation
for many on our street.

An inch or so of beer in a bowl,
with a compass rose
of lolly stick ramps
propped against the rim.

We set ours in the pantry.
53°N minus 3°E.

At times I'd lie awake, imagining
a line of roaches
marching blindly to their deaths,
in the malted well of *Dutton's* finest.

White Van

He'd seen some big skies in his time.
Even later, as secretary to the allotment association
he'd managed to get a good eyeful most days.

So, it came as a surprise when his health declined,
that he should want to close it out:
a little each day, until only a thin blue margin
in the curtains' folds,
betrayed the existence of a world outside.

He recalled how as a boy he'd been bedridden
with influenza and was given a book about
French explorers in the Mohawk valley.
He said he'd like to get hold of a copy.
He remembered watching his mum baking,
how he'd hook a currant from the bowl of sticky dough
with his forefinger, when she became obscured
by the sheets that hung like sails from the rack above.
He talked of sailing: his time in the R.A.F,

and he spoke of metaphysics:

of falling meteors bringing life to the seas.
How we're all constrained by gravity yet are
made up of energy: that life itself is weightless.
Death, he declared, releases stored energy into
the atmosphere where it amasses over time
to form stars and galaxies.

He talked openly of death – but didn't want to go there.
Towards the end he forced himself to stay awake,
afraid of being caught unawares.

They came for him in an unmarked white van.
We waited in the front room while they
carried him out. We watched him go.
At the brow of the hill where the houses ended
the sky fit snugly about him: a faded garment
he'd been reluctant to leave behind.

El Greco

The meals they couldn't sell usually
ended up on the 'specials' board:
from there – the soup.
The seats were tilted forward
so you didn't linger too long
after your dinner,
and the fruit machine
paid in tokens that could
only be used on the premises.
Yet minor inconveniences aside,
for the price of a cup of tea
there was no better place to hang out.
A meeting place at the end
of the precinct: a forum.
Dates arranged, disputes resolved,
shopping lists ticked off.
People coursed through its aisles,
eddying round prams and trolleys,
crossing junctions in rows of Formica tables.
You could meet a girl; or maybe pick
up a bargain from Fred the Bag
on his round of the pubs and cafes.
It was here I experimented with a purifying
tablet in a vinegar bottle, and was amazed
to see it turn clear as water.

Clear as the memory of how one day
the collective consciousness that
gravitates us towards a particular place,
waived; and I never went back.

Outcasts

Prolific: profligate,
they emulate the stars in their boldness
and intensity.
Unsung by poets, persecuted by gardeners,
the wrong type of flower
they stand defiant on the lawns and pathways
mid-Spring.
Outcasts, banished to the edgelands of our
towns and cities; flourishing on the sidings
and embankments: empty back-streets,
and the decaying monoliths of our industrial past.
Bouquets for the homeless.
In time the brash flowers transform
into opaque seed-heads: light, delicate
they await the breeze to stir.
Dandelion clocks.
Pluck one; take a breath and blow.
Count the hours – spread the joy.
Come Spring there'll be another starburst on the lawn.

Almanac

Ice

Cold-nosed cows wait.

The water bites.

I tilt and haul the wet disk
over the lip;

ease it down,

roll it to the side,

prop it by the fence:

leave it for the sun.

Economics

Once the head's through,
the rest falls out like jelly.
Twins: bull and heifer.
Statistically infertile.

I clear the airways
and present them to her.

She sniffs and nuzzles:
soft hair bristles as she lifts
the membrane with her tongue.

I wipe my hands on the grass and leave.
Later, they'll be taken away and shot.

First Cut

Refugees, islanders,
marooned:
the tall grass falling
like spent waves about them.

They weren't
expecting this.
Huddled in a rapidly
shrinking archipelago,
their homeland gone

it's a matter of time
before the exodus – of hares,
rabbits and mice, across an
empty field,
as the mower
takes its final run.

Haymaking

Blue sky, yellow field,
grey gatepost, red tractor,
green trailer.
Three laughing children:
six legs dangling.

Grey sky, blue field,
three tractors, green children,
five legs;
red gatepost, red trailer:
yellow scream.

Back end

White gulls stretch
pink worms
like tendons,
in the plough's wake.

It's the back end.
Low sun
burns intensely –
gives little warmth

Do not forget me!
It seems to cry:
spilling its dying embers
on the leaf litter.

Bowling with Sausage Kevin

In order to distinguish ourselves
from the inevitable collectives
of Marks, Pauls and Johns; we gave
each other nicknames, epithets.

I see those friends still – down at the local:
Scratch – formally Steven Itchin, talking
with Sky, the window fitter.
Flour-face the plasterer, Flash, the welder.
Dangerous Dave trying to drop his false teeth
in your pint – for a laugh.

Nuclear Dave sits quietly with a crossword,
his red face glowing by the window.
And there's Gibby, the horse whisperer: gypsy trader,
out on the green with his pint and talking horse;
trampling the crown, where Sausage Kevin
the local butcher, had just completed a round.

The Storm of October 2011

When the storm has passed,
copper birch leaves lie like loose
change on the pavement.

Bright offerings that deceive.
Money doesn't grow on trees.

Stamp Collecting

I was never an enthusiast as such.
Couldn't get excited over first day covers.
As an anodyne to rainy days and boredom,
I took up stamp collecting with my brother.
Chiefs, presidents, and fierce braided generals:
girls with garlands; palm trees by the sea.
A world within a 20p assortment
of used stamps from the former colonies.

Jamaica, Honduras, St Helena:
The Christmas Isles; New Zealand, Tanzania.
Exotic names – we'd board our ship in Blackburn,
embark, and moments later we'd be there.

Saw an Empire where the sun never set.
Returned as it descended on the West.

Revelation

It's World of Sport with Dickie Davies
and Big Daddy's about to unmask Kendo Nagasaki;
the mystical Japanese wrestler who doesn't speak
and never reveals his face.

I've waited all afternoon for this,

for years he's been feared and despised,
a malevolent hooded ghoul, taunting
the baying crowd: pouring scorn on his opponents
as he folds and pummels them like plasticine.

I imagined him at his samurai school,
enigmatic, steely, invincible;
his fights with warriors and Ninja; the strange rituals
and customs of his homeland – hara-kiri – kamikaze.

I imagined all these things, but mainly I
wondered what he looked like – I envisaged a fierce
oriental countenance with a scar on the left cheek;
more Genghis Khan than Hirohito.

It's been a long time coming.

The commentator's getting excited and I can barely
contain myself, as Big D forces him down: squeezes
his head in one hand like a grapefruit, reaches under
his chin and peels back the mask to reveal

Pete Thornley from Stoke on Trent.

The Chase

Returning later that evening,
I collected the pillow that bore his impression
and made my way up to the spare room.

Rolling my head into the cold crater,
I was overcome by the smell of decay.
Otherworldly, though in the circumstances

not unpleasant: like opening a book
that's stood undisturbed on a shelf for decades.
I closed my eyes and went to find him.

All routes were unfamiliar. Unsure of which
direction he'd taken, I eased myself
over a precipice and let myself fall

through impenetrable darkness; where faces,
some of whom I recognised, appeared out of the
inky blackness and vanished again like holograms.

Formless: a shadow within endless shadow,
I waded on. In time I developed gills; swam through
swamp heaving with the tangled limbs of mangrove.

Emerged into forest that was dense, and thick
with noises – but nothing. I was losing time; blindly
I began retracing my steps through the pathless night,

until a screech of tyres and the cushioned slam
of a car door, opened a portal bringing me back.
I turned the other way. Passed through woodchip

and lath and plaster, the skeletal timbers:
the speckled slate. It was then I caught sight of him.
This time chasing was hopeless; he was light

years away. Unfettered from gravity;
dazzling, bejewelled. Showering sparks on Orion's
Girdle: seeking an orbit encircling a sun.

Trial and Error

After ramming my stick
into a wasps nest,
came the realisation

that while I wasn't
allergic to their stings:
Pete was…

Primates

I *heard* them first – six men
laughing like maniacs when the brake slipped
and the platform slewed on its cable beneath the roof.

I dived for cover as the tools, clamps,
nuts and bolts came down four storeys
like a volley of live rounds on the warehouse floor.

Still they laughed when the floor gave way
and they clung, white-knuckled to the tubular frame;
the toothless brake fizzing down the hot wire.

With the carriage vertical and impact imminent
the hilarity intensified: whoops and shrieks,
loud guffaws.

The pulley snagged: a kink, a frayed strand of steel wire,
a bloody miracle? Two metres to ground and it snapped to a halt.
I helped steady it while they climbed down.

But they didn't see me – didn't see any of us.
Less raucous yet still giddy they huddled together
chattering like monkeys: a few playful cuffs and back-rubbing

before each going his own way. Crunching underfoot
the scattered fallout: finding a quiet place
to breathe, reflect; evolve.

Coleridge Street

Mick was getting nostalgic. 'You'd go down
the afternoon match and get your head kicked in,
then go down town at night and get filled in again.'
Mick Picup, darling of the secondary
picket: doyen of the Blackburn Trades Club.
Dissenter in a hotbed of dissent.
It was here the Beat poet Dave Cunliffe
urinated at the lectern, mid-stanza,
in protest at the local magistrates –
the masons and landowners who'd shut down
his small magazine for obscenities.
He'd published the word *cunt*, so they fucked him.

Mick got me thinking… We lived for the weekend.
Finish work Friday, put on your best gear,
then head down the Brow to the town centre,
where everyone was catered for: gays at
the Merchants, disco queens The Golden Palms:
at the Kings they held collections for
the I.R.A; while just around the corner
on the Barbary Coast punters could get
a knee-trembler by St Peter's steeple
from the street girls. Fighters to the Dun Horse,
pot smokers The Peel, bikers The Vulcan,
where one night I saw Viking Bill swing from
the curtains after winning thirty grand
on The Evening Telegraph's Cross the Ball.
Often we'd end up at seedy Cyril's
Top Hat Club, where hard men, hookers and general
misfits hung out for a late night session.
Its reputation made it exclusive;
in reality it was one of the safest
places to be – people put aside their
differences: everyone needed a drink;
there was usually a truce at the watering hole.

We were always on the lookout for girls.
For the most part the success rate wasn't great,
and we'd make our way back through the labyrinth
of terraces to Tim's place on Coleridge Street.
Occasionally we'd detour via
the Khyber Cafe; Blackburn's first curry house,
where our soft pink, delicate mouths were
seared by bhunas, madras and vindaloos
we'd select at random from a spattered menu.
Ring stingers we called them – burns you twice.
Back home we'd put on music and open
our wraps of hash – Lebanese red, Moroccan
black, Afghan gold: the names sounded exotic
and we'd ritually pass joints between us
with a reverential solemnity
that in itself betrayed our ignorance.

Come autumn we'd forage the magic mushrooms,
that rose on wet moorland above the town.
The trip house was on Lancaster Street.
Pale blue walls, a large rainbow adorning
the chimney breast, bean bags, lava lamps and
suspended speakers; we'd drink mushroom tea,
sit back, and settle in for the light show.
We were experimenting, pushing back
boundaries, opening up – we felt enlightened.
Off-season, we'd try acid in the form
of blotters or micro-dots. The effects
were similar, but the comedowns horrendous.
Desolation, emptiness a yearning,
as the trip wore off and we would head
back to Tim's through the iron grey morning.
Lying shivering in an upstairs room,
burnt out, yet wide awake: hurtling
along on a teeth grinding velodrome,
unable to get off – exhausted, sallow,
emaciated; hands seeming to shrivel and crawl;
strychnine screeching through our heads, through peak
and slow decay, we shook, desperate for sleep.

The pains of sleep.
                              'How was it for you?'
Eight hours later with a cup of tea
in the vacuous wasteland of Tim's kitchen,
we put on a brave face. 'Great, how about yourself?'

Our drug taking was sporadic: experimental.
Our drinking was prolific and established:
part of the culture. Blackburn was known
as the beeriest town in Britain, with a pub,
club or off-licence on nearly every street.
On my sixteenth birthday with my apprenticeship
looming dad took me to The Sportsmans
for a man to man, coming of age drink.
He put two pints on the table. 'Watch me,
it's not about getting drunk.' He lifted
his glass and took a slow, deliberate mouthful.
'Now your turn.' I'd been out drinking
the night before but this was different.
A ritual, which was about acceptance
and respect: from now on I'd be making
my own way. The farewell to adolescence
in the form of two pints of mild was profound.

'It's not the same anymore' Mick continued,
'there isn't the same sense of community
and solidarity we used to have,
where we felt we were all in it together.'
Typical trade union man: we may have
been doing similar things, but we weren't
cohesive: weren't   'all in it together.'
As kids we were territorial,
had our own areas and were always wary
when venturing alone into other parts
of the town: even as young adults we
tended to live within these areas.
It was only the town centre with its
pubs and shops; its hostels, bed-sits and
back-to-back terraces that remained neutral.

Over the next three decades, streets were bulldozed
and levelled, replaced with open greens,
pedestrian walkways, car parks, offices,
leisure centres and new road systems.
It's a brighter town now: greener, more airy.
No longer hemmed in by walls of houses
the intersection wind alters its pitch
as it funnels through and up into the valley
remembering...*the Somewhat that had been
imaginative lies, like a Cold Snuff
on the Circular Rim of the Candle-
stick, without even a stink of Tallow
to remind you that it was once cloathed
and mitred with Flame.*

Night Shift

Jim Riding hasn't slept for thirty years.
His body trips-out for ten minutes, then
the lights come on and he's away again.
He's seen more sunrises than most.
Keeps an eye on shifting constellations.
Eases himself through quiet days
and the long raucous nights, when inanimate
household objects make themselves heard.

Light bulbs hum like sub-stations.
Spoons ring, before settling at table.
A scratching pen sounds like mice in the loft.
The clock beats time:

                      a pick at a coalface,
hammering hard at the stubborn seam;
thumping, thumping till the light breaks through.

P
u
r
s
u
i
t

The
more elusive
she's become, the
more I long for her.
My float bobs on the
mirrored surface; while
my lure – a scrag-end –
dangles seductively,
stroking the reed bed
in the gentle current.
My intentions
while
not
altogether
honourable
are entirely natural.
I   yearn   and   wait...

Tick

It was said of Simon: for every good turn,
he'll do you two bad ones.

We shared a room in Munich.
Scrubbed pots by day,

then at night while I slept, he went
through my pockets, helping himself.

Fifty marks here: a hundred marks there.
I thought I was going mad.

Too young – too trusting;
got right under my skin.

Bled me dry then dropped off: disappeared.
Turned up thirty years later

selling lingerie on Bolton market.
I stayed clear in case he attached himself again.

Spartacus

How can the bird that is born for joy,
Sit in a cage and sing.

William Blake

He'd had a hard time.
His cage companions –
the limed finches
captured in the roosting trees,
had no concept
of walls and ceilings:
no idea how to behave
in a confined space.
The din, the commotion,
as they'd periodically
launch themselves
at the steel wire – and him,
who'd been incubated in a box
and knew nothing else.
Bruised and battered;
I was asked to take him in.

I hung his cage from
a beam by the skylight,
where he could see the
tree-tops, the changing
palette of days, silver moons
and distant constellations.
I wedged a cuttlefish
bone between the bars
for calcium, and,
(on the advice of the bird-catcher)
mixed dope seeds in
with his food to encourage
him to sing.
I called him Spartacus:
there is after-all,
something in a name…

I left the door open.
Being free-spirited
myself, I couldn't bear
to lock him up.
He'd been institutionalised:
a lifer, and it'd be
some days before he took
those first tentative
steps – a fledgling
easing out across the bough,
remaining in sight
of the nest.
His rehabilitation was
going to take time.
He lacked lift and flapping
wildly would descend
to the floor or furniture,
landing awkwardly
with his wings splayed.
He persevered

until the chairs, tables,
lampshade and sink,
became as the rocks,
trees and pools of the forest
he'd never known.
He sang his heart out.
I could relate: having
experienced the same
sensation myself, when I left
the cooped confines
of home, beginning
a journey that would
take me to Africa and
the farthest reaches
of the planet.
It's all about self-belief.

The walls of the cricket club
were topped with broken glass.
As kids we'd crush and
grind the shards with
stones making perches
to sit and watch the match.
His preferred spot
was a rail across
the kitchen window,
overlooking the pitch
and park, with its large
Victorian conservatory
where exotic trees
heaved and pressed the
wrought iron trusses
and glass roof,
in search of the sun.
Beside it stood an aviary.

On Sunday mornings
when the air was still,
before pealing church bells
anointed the streets, their
song eased under
the eaves: drifted in through
cracks and vents, stirring
something primal
within him.
He knew their language
and called back in joyous
self-awareness.
The flat was large.
I'd leave the interior
doors open.
He became adept at flying.
Kept me at arm's length.
I understood – a room
shrinks with familiarity.
I left him to it.

There's a lot to be said
for a name...
While I doubt he planned
his escape, he didn't
pass up the opportunity
when a friend left
the bathroom window ajar.
I'd been fearful of releasing
him in case he'd come
to harm, but was all for
self-determination:
quietly wished him well,
but left the window open a few
days in case he changed
his mind.
He never did.

I liked to think of him
living among the palms
and acacia in the hothouse:
conducting the Sunday choir.
Maybe settling down
and having a family –
As I did, until our world
became restricted and we
moved apart.
He'd felt safe in his
cage and had I never
opened the door
would've known no better.
With choice comes curiosity
and desire;
but it's never enough.

Beyond each horizon is
another – another after
that and then another,
until we eventually
return to our place
of embarkation: weary,
but in the knowledge
that without
fixed points of reference
we're liable to walk in circles.
My own world has shrunk to this:
a quiet room with books
and an open window.
These days it's the scene of
my greatest journeys.

The Photograph

Sunrise skims the distant ebbing tide.
Hunched figures at the waterline revealed,
as cockle-gatherers with suction boards,
that pad the spongy sand and tease
the creatures out from underneath.

The man, who stakes his nets by ancient right.
A farmer of the sea, and not the land.
Drives out to haul his catch in from the night.
The pier's exposed backbone rattles
out across the sand.

Deckchairs lashed to railings, shuttered booths.
A solitary gull gives out a cry; and
passing hangs her lyric on a bar,
which holds the note suspended in
an empty hollow sky.

Then stillness, but for occasional gusts;
clattering cables, loose on poles and boats.
Slowly though in unison,
landladies loose their charges, from
their gaily painted fronts.

Now all the town's awake – yet I'm alone.
A memory, on this ghostly promenade.
The youngster in the fading monochrome:
holding a monkey, with his brothers at his side;
on holiday in Morecambe circa 1965.

Glue

Without meaning to
sound trivial. The donkeys –
did they find a home?

Who Killed Fatima Durrani?

The Elders in the courtyard who condemned her.
The neighbour that accused her, gave her name.
The clerk who signed and sealed her life asunder.
The adulterer, who let her take the blame.

Was it the bullet, from a factory in France,
Whose coated casing came from Germany.
The lead tip, from a smelter in Murmansk.
The primer charge that came from Italy.

The cartridge powder came from Venezuela.
The rifle stock, from the U.S.A.
The barrel came from ore mined in Australia.
The firing-pin was made in the UK.

The man who pulled the trigger was a local.
An illiterate, who couldn't write his name.
Someone murdered Fatima Durrani.
So, tell me – *Who's* to Blame?

The Evergreen Nursing Home

The light is so much brighter here,
the air sweeter, the colours more vibrant;
flaming azaleas, wallflowers, marigolds,

lily of the valley: at the centre of the lawn
a shedding magnolia lays a wreath around
itself. Sounds amplify in the vacuous

stillness; an alighting bee reverberates like
a Triumph Bonneville, as he hauls himself between
flowers, his panniers bulging with nectar.

A scent of apple blossom: a peal of bluebells.
The patio door is open to the dayroom where
residents drowse and slumber. Beside them,

undrunk cups of tea and plates of biscuits
sit on lace doilies, waiting: Victoria sponge,
half empty glasses of lemonade. So silent

a scraping chair can open a chasm.
Death occupies the stoop; there'll be an empty place
at the breakfast table tomorrow morning.

Tonight, a light breeze will lift the blossom from
the apple tree and lay it across the lawn:
stir the magnolia wreath; its petals

scattered about like abandoned, upturned boats;
or sailing – a fleet of majestic gondolas
on a silvery moonlit lake.

Pilgrims

All who wander, are not lost.
$\qquad\qquad$ Mark Twain

You hold these places.
You fix them,
$\qquad\qquad\qquad$ yet they move.

You give them meaning.

Bearers of joy, grief, hope and despair.

Emotional junkyards.
$\qquad\qquad\qquad$ Out of sync,
$\qquad\qquad$ out of time.

$\qquad\qquad$ Memory the sorcerer.

Am I still here?

He keeps up a lot easier these days.
Back then I'd have to coax him,
ease him along the path.

Without breaking step, we round
the point and head down to the foreshore.

I've known him all my life, yet,
I see him differently now.

Wizened and curious,
if somewhat otherworldly?

Time-traveller. Mystic. Holy man.
A pilgrim with a floating map of faded meridians
and misplaced coordinates.

Here and there, then and now.

Rocky pathways, mist and foam.
Blackened stacks and terraced streets.
Hammered plate, crushed ore.

Fissures and gullies,
cut deep into his leathered skin.
His story.
A record of a journey.
The contours of a life unravelling.

I watch him as the scene dissolves
and he strains to scan the shoreline for the boy:
short-trousered pioneer, intrepid explorer,
strafed with sand and mud;

scrambling barefoot over barnacled boulders.
Gaping into rock pools.
Scavenging the tideline for chandlery,
fishing gear, ground glass and porcelain.
Wild with impulse and curiosity.

I've brought him here in search of the missing link.
The metaphorical clasp binding the past
to the present, the child to the man.

I'm desperate. He looks through me:
confused, agitated, unable to find the boy
among the rocks; or see him
in the size twelve boots that press the sand alongside.
He makes to leave.

Tar black shadows pollute
the landscape. The river creeps
like mercury. Pressure drops.

Doubt sets in.

This is a place for hermits and outcasts.
Joyless, impenetrable, desolate.

Storm clouds, iron grey, muscular,
buffer Black Coombe's looming peak.
He hears their voices,
knows their dialect: the forge
and anvil, furnace, steam press,
and smelting stack.

They speak of the rope walk and goods yard,
dry docks and channel dredgers, diesel turbines,
rolling stock.

Gas torches, rivet guns; the gates
where six generations passed, while soot
from the chimneys fell, large as snowflakes
and the town lolled in an ebony sheen.

I remain still, until he's seen enough.
Taking him by the arm, I lead him away.

The snow vacates its winter parish in the fells.
Surging melt waters proclaim their departure
through the hollow valley.

The river empties its charge.

Life reaffirms itself.

The sea holds the past;
and it's on these solitary walks, and within these silent
reveries,
I'm most likely to find him.

He's there now,
                                between the shoreline and horizon:
wandering through a mirage of factories and alleyways,
family dinners, Union meetings,
fishing trips and school sports days.

        Teacher, mentor,
ageless, timeless, he glides across the shimmering mosaic –

and vanishes.

The Polish Shop

Language is the only homeland
                                    Czeslaw Milosz

I'm in among the pickles and preserves.
Verdant rows of gherkins and olives,
fermented cabbage and stuffed vine leaves.
Shades of green, broken by colour bursts
of bright yellow sweet corn, scarlet paprika,
golden apricots mandarins and pears.

The food is familiar enough, though the labels
aren't corresponding to my own palette.
Korniszony, Oliwki, Kapusta, Slodka Kukurydza, Morele.
"Same food as English, with Polish names"
The manager explains helpfully.
"It tastes better in your own language."

He has a point, it's not just the visuals.
Rather, the words and their associations
that arouse and stimulate the senses.
Here, in this home away from home,
obiad z pleczonej wolowiny evokes the same
warmth and familiarity as a 'roast beef dinner'.
Sos pours like 'gravy' on the Sunday roast.
And *brzoskwinie i krem* carries the refreshing
summer taste of 'peaches and cream'.

Names, indelibly fixed in a place and time.
When I hear the word *trifle,* I'm back at
my grandparents on Ferguson Street.
The gingham tablecloth, grandad in the armchair
puffing his pipe. Sedate, soporific: the floral carpet,
the china cabinet, the crucifix on the wall.
Then, mention *shepherd's pie* and I'm home.
Ensconced on the sofa with a tray on my lap:
pushing a fork through a crimped, toasted potato lid;
releasing steam through buttery vents.

Alone in the aisle the decades slip by.
I'm lifting and coasting through the lexicon now.
Chocolate eclairs, iced buns, pilchards, Carnation milk.
Afternoon tea with relatives, long deceased.
All whistling kettles, ash buckets and mangles.

I see my fellow shoppers' tender cuts of *mięso*
and sweet, sticky *budynie,* subconsciously returning
them to their firesides of Krakow and Warsaw.
Our lives running parallel, separated only by the
shape and sounds of words; the memories they inform.
Language is the closest place to home.

Crude

When the embargo lifts, Mr Braithwaite trades
his black, fin-tailed Zephyr 6 for a Ford Cortina.
'Gas guzzler,' he tells us by way of explanation.
'Ten to the gallon on a good run:
barely enough to get you across town and back.'

A litany of names enter the common
lexicon, and make their way to the schoolyard.
Brent ——, Piper Alpha, Red Adair, Yom Kippur.
What could it mean, and where does all this plastic
come from?

Forming everything from biscuit-boxes and
pop bottles, to clothing, furniture and electronics:
video cassettes, tape recorders, digital watches.

In the classroom, calculators replace the abacus.
Black, sleek and futuristic, they do the work for you.
Solve equations; answer tricky questions.
Turn on the display: enter digits 71077345

Read upside down.

Haboob

The poetry class at the Asylum and Refugee Centre

I'm seeking out the common ground;
That piece of manicured lawn, barren scrub,
metalled road or corrugated shack
where we can meet.
These things shift – I'm flexible.
As a boy, believing there was room at the top,
I took the night bus to Monte Carlo.
My first encounter, an angry waiter.
I couldn't understand why he would expect
15% for walking five metres with a coffee.
He couldn't understand what I was doing there!
He had a point.

Two years later; a dormitory with refugees in Istanbul.
A place of shadows, the bare yellow bulb
illuminating the communal pot which bubbled and steamed
on a gas ring. Dignity amid the poverty.
Three decades on, I walked with the future King
over DC's hallowed turf.
We spoke of the environment: a shared burden.

When selecting poets for the class I avoided
confessionals, taking a lead from Burns,
whose first-person narrative was a collective *We:*
giving voice to the smallest, insignificant and reviled.
A common ground.

The students begin to write.
One man is reluctant, his pen poised,
he's overwhelmed, intimidated,
by the blank sheet of paper.
He's crossed mountains and deserts, been half-starved
and almost suffocated in sealed containers.
This is different.
He stares at the page, and goes nowhere.

MIGRANT! REFUGEE! ASYLUM SEEKER! FREELOADER!

It's a bad time to get blown up on these shores.

She sits with a group of women in the Hall
embroidering a tapestry. She's safe here, free
to make her own choices: her previous life,
always someone else's.

That took away her education.
Beat her, abused her every night,
and gave her daughter to an old man.
She escaped: smugglers offered help, then let her down;
took all she had – betrayed her:
sank the dinghy, leaving her to drown.

She concentrates on her embroidery.
Each staggered stitch a refugee.

****

The street furniture's had a reshuffle.
Cooling towers, gas tank, breweries and factories,
whose blackened stacks punctuated the town
with exclamation marks; replaced with housing,
retail parks, industrial units and mosques.
The old narrative broken, a new one emerging.

I'm becoming a minority – I always was?
Non-partisan Remainer, hopeless optimist:
accepting of change but saddened by the loss.

In Blackburns up and down the country,
amongst the poor white working class,
the resentment is palpable.
Ignored and overlooked
the estates mirror each other.
Booze Buster, bookies, and nail bar;
the proliferation of St George's flags,

tied to fences, bolted to sills and stretched across
bedroom windows.
A last stand. A community under siege.
The plucky Brits at Rourke's Drift holding out.

Poverty, resentment, patriotism,
a *Boys Own* view of British history – a combustible mix.
Something had to give.

****

It moves through town and city,
blowing up our streets and through our courtyards.
Passing through windows, under doors,
creeping into our houses, choking, suffocating.

What a difference a year makes.
How quickly priorities change.

****

Back in class we're discussing allegory.
How you can say one thing, yet mean something else:
the art of concealment.
The reluctant student begins to write.
From right to left, his Arabic script breaks
like gentle waves across the surface.
He's free now, no longer afraid.
There is still somewhere to hide.

The Crown

Walney Island

Crowns, sovereigns, golden guineas.
Currencies of the realm:
symbols of Imperial power.

Across the water a self-proclaimed King
lords over his duck pond.
A Parliament of Fowls.

Here, in this republic of gulls:
herring, black-backs, gannets;
ferocious, territorial, yet familial.

Treeless, windswept and exposed,
you can't be a stranger.
This is no axle on a sixteen-wheeler,

no socket in the landing gear.
Out here there is no place to hide,
yourself or your feelings:

you've got to be honest.
The Crown isn't brighter than the sun.
But it does endure.

Decorations

Beside the lake, beneath the trees

It's that time of year again.
The equinox has passed
and the sun's pale yolk
lingers into the evening.
Blackthorn blossoms
in the hedgerows where
songbirds weave the detritus
from winter storms
into nests for their young.
Daffodils garland the lake;
proclaim the Spring.

The days seem endless
as the canopy unfurls.
Dog walkers arrive lakeside:
pilgrims to Wordsworth's shrine,
to take it all in and decorate
the shoreline and trees
with their offerings.
Baubles of dog shit in
knotted sandwich bags,
strung out to fester;
greet the local and visitor alike
on the wooded paths.

It ruins it for me.
Away from here I can
think of little else.
For oft' when on my couch I lie…
They flash upon that inward eye…

Skenner

A curtain of hair, a cupped hand.
It wasn't so much the squint but rather the efforts
I went to conceal it, that obscured my view in childhood.

'Skenner!' they'd shout in the schoolyard, or whisper,
  through the long-drawn-out Sundays at the chapel.

There's independence in isolation.
Self-conscious became self-aware,
self-contained: determined.

Dad tipped up his wage for the operation.
The boys noticed.
Beauty queen: showgirl; Miss Lovely Legs –
And, after a chance meeting at Blackburn station:
a first-class ticket to America.

The view just got better.

Crows

They don't come here by crow;
yet they wear the night well.
The inky shadows of the hedgerows:
the unlit lane.

They don't come here by crow;
but the scattered crumbs of pleasure –
throbbing beats: a 'Come fuck me' look
from a stranger, sustain.

They don't come here by crow;
though the black-tied doorman leaves
carrion in the carpark. The unlucky,
the unwise. Mind your step

Magic Lantern

Streaks of silver sunlight on the frosted field.
Silver flecks on the dormant blackthorn.
A flash of white light on the window-pane, and I'm back;
walking with my mother along the row of fish stalls,
glistening brilliantine against the soot-black gable
of the old town hall.

Blown inland each market day. Bonneted and shawled:
otherworldly; the wide-eyed john dorys, hooded monkfish,
flat-faced flounder and gnarled, crusted oysters
peddled their wares. 'Us 'usbands 'ave catched 'em!'
They shout.   I'm holding tight to my mother's hand
as we move down the row.
Then they're gone: back to the sea; back to another time.
My mother too slips her grip, and I'm alone once more.

It's like that with memory. The seemingly random triggers
that turn the magic lantern; taking you back, drawing you in.

They leave, but they don't go far.

My boy Adam. Gold in his hands, and heart.
Dorothy, who showed me glamour then died as her child was born.
John, Tom, Dad. Anchors, rocks and pillars. My metaphors.
And towers –
Not reaching the heavens.
Just trying to see that little bit further down the road.
To another place: a better place.

Portrait in Black

It's in these, the quiet months,
the winter months,
that the stooped form of my mother
appears on the chimney-breast
above the hearth,
when I rise from the chair.
Slightly hesitant,
she steadies herself,
before edging her way along the wall
and disappearing behind the drapes,
as I leave the room.

She'll be there when I re-enter.
Peering out,
a little tentative at first;
then stepping clear and easing
her way back along
the wall, before
tucking herself in behind the armchair
as I take my seat beside the fire.
I'll be chaperoned this way
until early spring, when she'll depart.
Returning in late autumn.
A little more hunched.
A little more hesitant.
Easy does it…

Book Reviews

Thunder Alley,

Mark Ward works in Grasmere, tending to the grounds of Dove Cottage. He was born in Blackburn but is widely travelled and has done interesting jobs in far-flung places. This collection is principally located in his home town and takes its title from one of its streets. There is nothing of the professional northerner about Ward, nor does he play to any northern stereotype. The angle of his poems is always straight. He doesn't do anything tricksy or clever-clever. He doesn't play the poetic chameleon. I'm reminded of Einstein comparing Beethoven with Bach and saying the latter was almost pure music while the former was dramatic, almost personal. You could say Ward writes a Bach-like poem: it seeks for purity of expression. Its leathery language wants to force out the personal, the dramatic so that a near purity of expression allows them their place outside the poem. There's a poem called *The Mansion of Aching Hearts* which exemplifies this:

> *At the former Union Workhouse on the hill,*
> *they'd sit in soporific bliss and stare*

The lines are attractively rhythmical and the sibilants of the second carefully chosen but unobtrusive. Ward has that capacity to weave in clever poetic uses without drawing attention to them. You can read the poem without noticing them, just as its meaning is subtle as a gentle smile. It's typical of Ward's capacity to suck significance into a poem and to hold it within the solid bricks and mortar of a robustly built piece. The workhouse is a metaphor for a set of social relations long since surpassed but whose legacy we still endure. But this is a former workhouse its poor inmates replaced by the mad and mentally defective till its closure. The tact of the poem is to withhold the flood of questions and doubts it engenders. The ghosts of the Victorian poor and the shades of the distressed minds no-one knew how to deal with or wanted to acknowledge haunt this beautiful poem. Not all the poems are as memorable as this. There are some almost throwaway pieces; *Regret vi* for example. The collection might have been better without them but they don't mar in any real way. My guess is they were included for change of tone and to introduce humour. He can be effectively funny, as the *Regret* poems (there are ten of them) show. *Spanish Lament* for example nicely spikes how things that seem to change often remain the same, a good lesson in our spectacular (in the Debordian sense) society; but a piece like *Cycles* shows his real talent. I would say a social historian of the future wanting to understand what happened to the British sensibility in the years after 1979 might well be advised to start with this poem. In fourteen lines he sums up all that is meant by *dumbing down, the broken society, feral youth, cultural coarsening* and many more fairly impotent clichés of our time. We are, of course, in denial about what Ward is exploring here. We are supposed to believe it is a marginal phenomenon; but the poem gets it right: we all know this viciousness is now central to how we relate to one another, however various its forms. *Shadows* too is an excellent poem about danger, abuse and the perilousness of innocence. It exemplifies Ward's quiet, reserved, concentrated style. When he lapses from this he becomes less individual but it is a high achievement that, though his work is not radically different in means from that of many contemporary poets, he has succeeded in finding a territory, which though not extensive is recognisably his own.

Alan Dent. *MQB*

Coleridge Street
Review. Summer 2013

Coleridge Street is in Blackburn, a once thriving Lancashire mill town now pretty much a no-man's land between Preston, which has risen on its university (money and cosmopolitanism), and the backwaters of east Lancashire where you can buy a house for ten grand and are unknown to the smart kids making their way in New New Labour. Mark Ward chooses the name of the street for the title of this pamphlet from **Aussteiger Publications,** because he comes from Blackburn and now works in the Lake District. The long title poem is a delightful experiential time-travelogue through the streets, pubs, clubs and front rooms of the town in the adolescent years. It pricks the illusory bubble of small-town dullness and inactivity:

there's as much going on here as in Chelsea or Islington, it just goes on without so much money. Ward's writing is clear, tight and creates the right pace of movement. His references are charming, hilarious, wry and sometimes tragic. He mentions Dave Cunliffe, that small press veteran of the town, hounded by the authorities, who rightly deserves celebration for his tenacity and lack of conventional ambition. In hundreds of small towns across Britain, young people have found a way to make their lives exciting in spite of the efforts of the official culture to dull them down. Good for them, and good for Mark Ward. In the title poem, as in others in this little book, he cultivates a garden of sturdy poetic plants; they are beautiful, benodorous, they make you smile and cheer you up. This is a collection to carry in your pocket and to take out on the bus (in Blackburns up and down the land) on the train, in waiting rooms or during those long minutes in the modern day first circle, the meeting. It is small and short but its contents are big and enduring.

Alan Dent: *MQB*

Review.
A Guide to Historic Haworth & the Brontës, by Mark Ward with Ann Dinsdale and Robert Swindells

In response to the need for a popular guide to Haworth, local poet and tour guide Mark Ward, Brontë Parsonage Museum librarian, Ann Dinsdale, and award-winning children's writer Robert Swindells, have combined to produce this handy guide to Haworth and its most famous inhabitants. The book is structured around four walks: one long (7 miles: Top Withens, circular) and three short (1 ¼ miles: Penistone Hill; ¾ mile: Parsonage, Church and Village Top; and 500 metres!) Within each walk we are introduced to a rich mixture of Haworth history. The Brontës have a prominent place of course, and have an additional chapter by librarian Dinsdale on The Brontës of Haworth, but Haworth's history neither stopped nor started with the Brontës. Thus in the Penistone stone quarries we learn about the ancient sea beds of the Carboniferous period which gave rise to a prosperous local quarry industry; on our moorland walk we learn about the changing patterns of farming and how the appearance of the moors has changed over time; we learn about the mills, the

Luddites, and something about the lives of those who are buried in the churchyard. In Bob Swindells's tongue-in-cheek 500 metre walk, we learn of the feature film cowboy Tom Mix and aviator Amy Johnson.

The writing is clear – the background to Grimshaw and the Evangelical Revival is masterfully encapsulated in three sentences – but the strength of the book is that it gives the background to what we can still see – once we have been told where to look! The times I've walked, unknowingly, over Tom Mix's flagstone, passed the air shafts of underground passages near Dimples Lane, and under the Celtic head in North Street! Not only is this an excellent and robust little guide for the visitor to Haworth today, but it also reminds us of the Haworth that has passed, the Haworth that the Brontës knew, from Brandy Row and the horse fairs on Penistone Slack, to the then-busier moors, and the treacherous bogs, the Isolation Hospital at Upper Heights Farm, and the packhorse trails.

The work concludes with a list of Places to Stay. This is an excellent little gem for the visitor. RD, *Brontë Society Transactions, The Journal of Brontë Studies*

Acknowledgements

Many of these poems have been published in books, pamphlets, newspapers and journals and/or have been commissioned, exhibited, and broadcast on radio and TV. These include two collections: *Thunder Alley* Aussteiger Publications 2008, *reissued* Penniless Press Publications 2014, and *The Visitor's Book*, Penniless Press Publications 2014. The pamphlets *Coleridge Street*, Aussteiger Publications 2012 and *Portrait in Black*, Lodestar Publications 2017. With individual poems appearing in journals *The Crazy Oik, MQB, State of the Arts,* and the Wordsworth Trust's *Messenger.*

The *Polish Shop* and *Haboob* were commissioned by Blackburn Museum & Art Gallery for its *Kick Down the Barriers* exhibition. They were recorded for BBC Radio Lancashire. *Haboob* was published by

ARC Asylum & Refugee Centre for National Refugee Week 2020. *The Polish Shop* was published in State of the Arts.

Skenner, Crows, Magic Lantern and *Portrait in Black* featured in the *Lodestar Exhibition* at The Bureau Centre for the Arts, Blackburn, along with the publication *Portrait in Black*.

The Crown was commissioned by The Crown Hotel in association with Signal Film & Media, Barrow in Furness, Cumbria.

The Photograph and *Glue* formed part of the exhibition Five Rivers in Morecambe, Lancashire and featured in a pamphlet of the same name,

Pilgrims was commissioned by photographer Phil Green for a series exploring dementia.

Junction 31 was shortlisted in the International Sonnet Competition and published in the anthology *Hand Luggage Only*, Open Poetry Ltd 2007

The collection *Thunder Alley* was a winner in the BBC Reading Detectives series. It was shortlisted in the International Poetry Book Awards 2021

Oh, and by the way, featured in *Accents* ITV Granada Reports 2017

I would like to take this opportunity to personally thank the following people for their support: My publisher Ken Clay at The Penniless Press, Neil Rollinson, Paul Farley, Kate Davis, David Moore, Annalie Talent, Alan Dent, Pamela Woof, Jenny Uglow, Catherine Kay, Graham Ward, and Chrissie Spencer at Blackburn with Darwen Council.

Author Photograph: Annalie Talent